ALGERIA: HUMAN RIGHTS

EXECUTIVE SUMMARY

Algeria is a multi-party republic whose head of state and government (the president) is elected by popular vote for a five-year term. The president has the constitutional authority to appoint and dismiss cabinet members and the prime minister. There are no presidential term limits, and President Abdelaziz Bouteflika has been in office since 1999. The legislative elections held in May 2012 did not result in significant changes to the composition of the government. Foreign observers characterized the elections as largely peaceful, but noted low voter turnout and a high rate of ballot invalidity. Security forces, reporting to civilian authorities, maintained stability and order throughout the voting process.

The three most significant continuing human rights problems were restrictions on freedom of assembly and association, lack of judicial independence, and overuse of pretrial detention.

Other human rights concerns were limitations on the ability of citizens to change their government, excessive use of force by police, and poor prison conditions. Widespread corruption accompanied reports of limited government transparency. Women faced violence and discrimination, and the government maintained restrictions on workers' rights.

Impunity for police and security officials remained a problem, as the government did not publicly provide information on actions taken against officials accused of wrongdoing.

Abuses by illegal paramilitary forces (terrorists) remained a significant problem. Terrorist groups committed a significant number of attacks against government officials, members of security forces, and civilians.

On January 16, approximately 40 terrorists affiliated with former al-Qa'ida in the Islamic Maghreb (AQIM) leader Mokhtar Belmokhtar (under the name Those Who Sign in Blood) entered Algeria from Libya and attacked two transport buses carrying employees from a natural gas plant near In Amenas. Additional gunmen then stormed the plant and its residential quarters, rigging the facility with bombs and taking a total of 800 hostages, including 132 foreign nationals, for four days. The gunmen reportedly searched for foreign plant employees door to door, affixed explosives around the necks and waists of some hostages, and expressed intent to transport the hostages to Mali. The standoff ended on January 19, two days after Algerian Special Forces launched an attack on the facility. Terrorists killed one Algerian and 39 foreign hostages from nine countries, including three American citizens. Algerian military strikes on the facility killed 29 attackers, and Algerian authorities captured and took into custody three attackers. At the end of the year the surviving attackers remained incarcerated awaiting trial.

Section 1. Respect for the Integrity of the Person, Including Freedom from:

a. Arbitrary or Unlawful Deprivation of Life

On September 13, a 25-year-old man in the town of Boucherka died after visiting a police station. The man, known only by the initials "AK," entered a local police station to inquire about a fine he received. He departed the station with severe head injuries and was taken to the hospital, where he died hours later. News of the incident sparked demonstrations throughout the town and the neighboring city of Jijel. Residents called the incident "suspicious." The national police conducted an investigation, but the results had not been made public by year's end.

Security services confronted terrorists affiliated with several groups including AQIM, the Movement for Unity and Jihad in West Africa (MUJAO), and Those Who Sign in Blood. Media reports indicated that security services killed approximately 150 suspected terrorists in the course of firefights and raids during the year.

b. Disappearance

Reported disappearances were generally instances of individuals apprehended by security forces and held for several days before their families were notified or they were released. In all cases during the year, security services indicated that the individuals were suspected of terrorism or terrorist collusion.

On March 22, the UN Human Rights Committee found that Algeria violated the International Covenant on Civil and Political Rights in the cases of two disappeared individuals: Farid Mechani, arrested in 1993 by plain-clothed police officers in Algiers and later tried *in absentia* on terrorism-related charges by an Algiers court; and Djamel Saadoun, arrested in 1996 by gendarmerie officials on the charge of failure to comply with a conscription notice after he disappeared from a military training camp. The committee instructed the government to provide effective remedies to the remaining family members of Mechani and Saadoun. At year's end these remedies had not been met.

Armed individuals conducted abuses against civilians, including kidnappings, false checkpoints, and extortion, particularly in areas east of Algiers and in the southern portion of the country. Security services reported that approximately 15 persons were kidnapped from the area in 2013, some for ransom. Figures on total ransom payments were unavailable.

According to Abderahmane Arrar, president of Algeria's National Association for the Defense of Children (NADA), 1,300 cases of child abduction and disappearance were reported during the year, including 50 in the city of Algiers.

c. Torture and Other Cruel, Inhuman, or Degrading Treatment or Punishment

The law prohibits torture, but nongovernmental organizations (NGOs) and local human rights activists alleged that government officials sometimes employed torture and abusive treatment to obtain confessions. Government agents can face prison sentences of between 10 and 20 years for committing such acts, and some individuals were tried and convicted. There were no reported cases of prosecution of security service officials during the year. The government maintains internal lists of prosecutions and convictions of security officials. Local and international NGOs asserted that impunity was a problem.

Amnesty International (AI) maintained that security forces operated "unrecognized detention centers where detainees were at risk of torture or other ill-treatment."

Prison and Detention Center Conditions

Physical Conditions: Prison conditions generally did not meet international standards, and the government did not permit visits by independent human rights observers to military, high-security, Intelligence and Security Department (DRS), or standard prison facilities or to detention centers.

In May the government reported the approximate total number of prisoners and detainees in prisons and detention facilities at 65,000, of which approximately 600 were women and 420 juveniles. The total number of prison beds was 75,000 in

131 facilities. Official government statistics published in August 2012 indicated that pretrial detainees moved from pretrial detention facilities to prisons to alleviate overcrowding accounted for approximately 10 percent of this total, but observers disputed that percentage. Some observers, including government-appointed human rights officials, attributed overcrowding in pretrial detention facilities to "excessive use" of pretrial detention.

Officials generally held male and female prisoners separately, with conditions reportedly better for women than for men. Officials held juveniles separately from adults. Pretrial detainees were generally kept in separate detention facilities co-located with police stations, but were occasionally moved to prisons due to overcrowding. Individuals detained as terrorism suspects were held at facilities administered by the DRS. Some individuals previously detained at these facilities claimed abuse by security service officers.

On July 22, the Laghouat branch of the Algerian League for the Defense of Human Rights (LADDH) released a communique alleging that conditions at Laghouat detention facility were substandard. The communique alleged that inmates were provided access to the outdoors only during the hottest afternoon hours of the day, that some inmates suffered from malnutrition, and that the facility was unhygienic.

Administration: Recordkeeping on inmates and detainees was substandard. The penal code permits the substitution of community service for imprisonment for nonviolent, first-time offenders whose crimes carry a maximum prison sentence of three years or less. No ombudsman exists to serve on behalf of prisoners or detainees. Prisoners can submit uncensored complaints to penitentiary administration and those in standard facilities are permitted weekly visits by family members, who are authorized to provide detainees with food and clothing. All Muslim holy days are observed within all prisons, and authorities permit prisoners to participate in religious events and provide them with prayer space.

Independent Monitoring: While the government allowed the International Committee of the Red Cross (ICRC) and local human rights observers to inspect low-security prisons and detention centers, it refused access to military and high-security prison and detention facilities. The ICRC conducted 142 visits in 2012 to 50 facilities and 5,443 detainees. On July 23, Minister of Justice Mohamed Charfi announced that since 2009, the Ministry of Justice (MOJ) gave 537 authorizations to media outlets to visit prisons, resulting in more than 1,000 media visits to prisons in the same time period. The same day the MOJ announced the dismissal of the director of Serkadj prison in Algiers and his assistant after Algerian television station Echourouk broadcast an interview with a detainee filmed with a hidden camera in violation of prison regulations.

AI reiterated concerns about the possibility of torture and abuse in uninspected, "unrecognized" detention facilities operated by intelligence and security services. Families of repatriated detainees were reportedly permitted to visit detainees held in temporary custody in these facilities.

Improvements: In March the Ministry of the Interior's General Directorate for Prison Administration and Resettlement (DGAPR) concluded a five-year prison reform project undertaken in collaboration with the British government and the International Center for Prison Studies (ICPS). The project resulted in the DGAPR's adoption of the ICPS "A Human Rights Approach to Prison Management" handbook and the establishment of five pilot prisons conforming to ICPS recommendations. The handbook was used as a primary training manual for prison management personnel at every level. On July 5, President Bouteflika pardoned 5,000 detainees convicted of misdemeanor-level crimes.

d. Arbitrary Arrest or Detention

Overuse of pretrial detention was a systemic problem, although there has been improvement in this area since the 2011 repeal of the country's emergency law. The government-appointed head of the National Consultative Commission for the Promotion and Protection of Human Rights (CNCPPDH), Farouk Ksentini, noted that authorities saw pretrial detention as an "implicit sign" of guilt. CNCPPDH expressed concern that judges refused 90 percent of detainees' applications for "judicial control," a type of pretrial liberty utilized in lieu of a bail system. Individuals detained as terrorism suspects are held at facilities administered by the DRS. Some individuals previously detained at these facilities claimed abuse by security service officers, but there was no evidence that physical conditions at these facilities were markedly worse than those at standard prison facilities.

Role of the Police and Security Apparatus

General responsibility for maintaining law and order is shared by the 60,000-member Gendarmerie Nationale, which performs police functions outside of urban areas under the auspices of the Ministry of National Defense, and the 130,000-member Surete Nationale, or national police force, organized under the Ministry of the Interior (MOI). The DRS is also organized under the Ministry of National

Defense, and its various units perform law enforcement functions related specifically to terrorism and national security.

Impunity remained a problem. The criminal code provides mechanisms to investigate abuses and corruption, but the government did not provide public information on disciplinary or legal action against police, military, or other security force personnel, citing morale and security concerns.

Arrest Procedures and Treatment of Detainees

According to the law, police must obtain a summons from the Prosecutor's Office to require a suspect to appear in a police station for preliminary questioning, but this was not uniformly done. Summonses also are used to notify and require the accused and the victim to attend a court proceeding or hearing.

Police may make arrests without a warrant if they witness the offense. Public lawyers reported that procedures for warrants and summonses usually were carried out properly.

The constitution specifies that a suspect may be held in detention for up to 48 hours without charge. If more time is required for gathering additional evidence, the police may request that the prosecutor extend the suspect's detention to 72 hours. Those suspected of terrorism or subversion may be held legally for 12 days without charge or access to counsel under the law. Confessions and statements garnered during this period – which may be extended by a prosecutor's application to a judge – are permissible to use in court. The initial court appearance of a suspect in terrorism matters is not public. At the end of the 12-day period, the detainee has the right to request a medical examination by a physician of choice within the jurisdiction of the court. Otherwise the judicial police appoint a doctor. The certificate of the medical examination is then entered into the detainee's file.

There is no system of bail. In non-felony cases and in cases of individuals involved in terrorism that have exceeded a 12-day period and any authorized extension, suspects often were released on provisional liberty referred to as "judicial control" while awaiting trial. Under provisional liberty status, suspects are required to report weekly to the police station in their district, reside at an agreed-upon address, and are forbidden to leave the country until a disposition is reached on the case.

Judges rarely refused prosecutorial requests for extending preventive detention, which by law can be appealed. Should the detention be overturned, the defendant has the right to request compensation.

Most detainees have prompt access to a lawyer of their choice, and the government provides legal counsel to indigent detainees. Some detainees were held incommunicado without access to their families or lawyers.

Arbitrary Arrest: Although the law prohibits arbitrary arrest and detention, authorities sometimes used vaguely worded laws to arrest and detain individuals considered to be disturbing public order. Both AI and the UN special rapporteur on freedom of speech criticized the country's law prohibiting unauthorized gatherings, calling for the law to be amended to require only notification as opposed to application for authorization. These observers, among others, pointed to the law as a significant source of arbitrary arrests intended to suppress activist speech. Police arrested protestors in Algiers and elsewhere in the country throughout the year for violating the law against unregistered public gatherings, but detainees were typically released the same day without charge.

Between March and May, security services arrested protestors in several southern Algerian cities (including Ghardaia and Ouargla) on charges of inciting unlawful gatherings. On March 26, police in Ghardaia arrested 18 protestors associated with the National Committee for the Defense of the Rights of the Unemployed (CNDDC) who demonstrated at the city's annual carpet fair. Following their May 27 arraignment, 10 of the protestors were released from custody, and the remaining eight were charged with offenses relating to incitement of an unlawful gathering.

On May 24, CNDDC protestors organized a sit-in outside of the Laghouat offices of the National Employment Agency to protest high unemployment. Police responded to the scene, detained ten protestors, and released them the same day.

On June 23, representatives of the Independent Youth Movement for Change were arrested at an Algiers cemetery while attempting to lay a wreath at the grave of former Algerian president Mohamed Boudiaf on the anniversary of his assassination. They were released from custody the same day.

Pretrial Detention: Prolonged pretrial detention remained a serious issue. Pretrial detainees were believed to comprise approximately 10 percent of the total detainee/prisoner population. The law does not provide a person in detention the right to a prompt judicial determination of the legality of the detention. AI continued to allege that individuals detained on security-related charges were sometimes held in excess of the 12-day prescribed period.

Detention of Rejected Asylum Seekers or Stateless Persons: There were reports that the government deported some asylum seekers after trials without legal counsel given to the applicant. Country representatives of the Office of the UN High Commissioner for Refugees (UNHCR) reported that authorities respected UNHCR refugee documentation and did not detain or deport individuals in possession of asylum seeker certificates.

e. Denial of Fair Public Trial

While the constitution provides for an independent judiciary, the president exercises supreme judicial authority, and the executive branch limited judicial independence. The judiciary was not impartial and was often subject to influence and corruption. The constitution provides for the right to a fair trial, but authorities did not always respect legal provisions regarding defendants' rights. The High Judicial Council is responsible for judicial discipline and the appointment of all judges. President Bouteflika serves as the president of the council.

Trial Procedures

The constitution provides for the right to a fair trial, but authorities did not always respect legal provisions regarding defendants' rights. Defendants are presumed innocent and have the right to be present and to consult with an attorney, provided at public expense if necessary. Most trials are public and all are nonjury. Defendants can confront or question witnesses against them or present witnesses and evidence on their behalf. Past reports indicated that courts occasionally denied defendants and their attorneys access to government-held evidence, but there were very few reports of such incidents during the year. Defendants have the right to appeal. The testimony of men and women has equal weight under the law.

Political Prisoners and Detainees

International and local observers alleged that anti-terrorism laws and restrictive laws on public assembly were used to detain political activists. On October 9, Algiers police arrested blogger Abdelghani Aloui, and on October 10 a court in Algiers charged him with incitement to terrorism. Aloui's supporters contended the charges were falsified and based on Aloui's posting of insulting caricatures of President Bouteflika to his Facebook page. On October 23, Algerian news website

Algerie Focus posted a video featuring a man bearing a strong resemblance to Aloui calling for jihad. Aloui's lawyer admitted the individual depicted in the video was his client, but contended the audio track had been altered. Aloui remained in custody during the preliminary phases of his prosecution.

Civil Judicial Procedures and Remedies

The judiciary was neither independent nor impartial in civil matters and lacked independence in some human rights cases. Family connections and status of the parties involved influenced decisions. Individuals may bring lawsuits, and there are administrative processes related to amnesty, which may provide damages to the victims or their families for human rights violations and compensation for alleged wrongs.

f. Arbitrary Interference with Privacy, Family, Home, or Correspondence

The constitution prohibits such actions, although government authorities infringed on citizens' privacy rights. According to human rights activists, the government monitored the communications of political opponents, journalists, human rights groups, and suspected terrorists. Security officials reportedly searched homes without a warrant. Security forces conducted unannounced home visits.

g. Use of Excessive Force and Other Abuses in Internal Conflicts

Killings: Government efforts continued to eliminate elements of AQIM, MUJAO, and Those Who Sign in Blood in Algeria. Reports from human rights and other groups indicated that security service officials killed approximately 150 individuals suspected of affiliation with and action on behalf of AQIM during the course of raids on strongholds and firefights.

Section 2. Respect for Civil Liberties, Including:

a. Freedom of Speech and Press

Although the constitution provides for freedom of speech and press, the government restricted these rights through accusations of defamation and informal pressure on publishers, editors, and journalists.

Freedom of Speech: Individuals were not able to criticize the government publicly. Citizens were arrested and detained for doing so, or practiced self-restraint in voicing public criticism. The law criminalizing speech about the conduct of the security forces during the internal conflict of the 1990s remained in force, although there were no cases of arrest or prosecution under the law during the year. The penal code provides for up to three years' imprisonment for tracts, bulletins, or flyers that "may harm the national interest" or up to one year for defaming or insulting the president, the parliament, the army, or state institutions.

Press Freedoms: The government imposed a complete information blackout during the January terrorist attack at the gas plant in the In Amenas. Media representatives harshly criticized the decision.

Many political parties, including legal Islamist parties, had access to the independent press and used it to express their views. Opposition parties also disseminated information via the Internet and published communiques. Journalists expressed frustration over the near-impossibility of receiving information from public officials. Print media outlets relied on the government for physical printing materials and operations. The government maintained a monopoly on broadcast media despite a decree permitting the operation of independent broadcast media outlets. There were no cases of government interference in book publication during the year.

On May 19, the chief prosecutor in Algiers announced that criminal charges related to threats to national security, unity, and stability had been filed against Hichem Aboud, editor of Algerian newspapers *Djaridati* and *Mon Journal*, following publication of articles in both papers alleging that President Bouteflika was in a "comatose" state. On June 26, authorities detained Aboud Houari Boumediene at the International Airport in Algiers while he attempted to board a flight to Tunis. He appeared before a judge in Algiers the following day and was advised that he was subject to movement restrictions under the law in light of the charges against him. On September 9, Aboud filed a complaint with the UN High Commissioner for Human Rights, accusing government authorities of violating his right to free expression. Aboud remained at liberty within the country pending trial.

On September 11, protestors gathered outside of the historic Algiers post office, a common location for demonstrations, to demonstrate against Western military action in Syria. Police dispersed the demonstration and arrested several participants and organizers, among them two journalists from Algiers daily *El Watan*. The journalists were taken to a police station on Avenue Didouche Mourad where they were held for approximately three hours before being released without charge.

<u>Violence and Harassment</u>: There were no reports of violence or harassment of members of the media, but the government did not take any specific steps to ensure the safety of journalists and the independence of the media.

<u>Censorship or Content Restrictions</u>: Major news outlets faced direct and indirect retaliation for criticism of the government. On May 18, the government ordered its printing house, which prints all Algiers newspapers, to cease printing Hichem Aboud's newspapers (*Mon Journal* and *Djaridati*) to avoid dissemination of an article on President Bouteflika's health. The law permits the government to censor imported books, but there were no cases in which the government exercised this authority during the year.

<u>Libel Laws/National Security</u>: NGOs and observers criticized the law on defamation as vaguely drafted and the definitions therein as failing to comport to internationally recognized norms. The law defines defamation as "any allegation or imputation of a fact offending the honor or consideration of a person, or of the body to which the fact is imputed." The law does not require that the fact alleged or imputed be false or that the statement within which it is contained be made with malicious intent to damage another individual's reputation. Defamation is not a crime, but carries high civil penalties ranging from DZD 100,000 to 500,000 ($1,250 to $6,250).

<u>Publishing Restrictions</u>: Individuals who wish to initiate regular publications must obtain authorization from the government. The law requires the director of the publication to hold Algerian citizenship. The law additionally prohibits periodicals from receiving direct or indirect material support from foreign sources.

<u>Actions to Expand Press Freedom</u>: The government ended its monopoly on broadcast media in September 2011, passing a law to permit private media companies access to radio and television airwaves. In July the Ministry of Communication approved three private television channels (Ennahar, el-Chourouk, and el-Djazairia) to open offices in Algiers. All three channels previously maintained offices abroad.

Internet Freedom

Access to the internet generally was unimpeded, although the government monitored e-mail and social media sites. Individuals and groups could engage in the expression of views via the Internet, including by e-mail. Intelligence services closely monitored the activities of political and human rights activists on social media sites such as Facebook. Several activists report that even the slightest misstep in a Facebook update could result in arrest and questioning.

On May 2, a court in Oran sentenced Algerian musician Faisal Bensalah (known professionally as Cheb Faisal) to a six-month suspended sentence and a fine of DZD 100,000 ($1,250) after his conviction for undermining the authority of a state institution. Authorities alleged that a song by Bensalah leaked on the internet contained lyrics insulting the police. Bensalah contested that music of his composition had been used with lyrics composed and recorded by another individual, that he did not compose or record the lyrics in question, and that he had no hand in uploading the song to the internet.

The law on cybercrime establishes procedures for using electronic data in prosecutions and outlines the responsibilities of service providers to cooperate with authorities. Under the law electronic surveillance operations may be conducted to prevent offenses amounting to terrorist or subversive acts and infractions against state security pursuant to written authorization from a competent judicial authority.

By law internet service providers face criminal penalties for the material and websites they host, especially if subject matters are "incompatible with morality or public opinion." The Ministry of Justice, the Ministry of Interior, and the Ministry of Post, Information Technology, and Communication Telecommunication have oversight responsibilities. The cybercrime law provides sentences of six months to five years in prison and fines between DZD 50,000 and DZD 500,000 ($625 and $6,250) for users who do not comply with the law, including the obligation to cooperate with law enforcement authorities against cybercrime.

Academic Freedom and Cultural Events

Academic freedom was generally restricted. Academic seminars and colloquia occurred with limited governmental interference, but there were delays in issuing visas to international participants and instances in which authorities denied international experts entrance. Participants and speakers invited to cultural and academic events whose biographies included references to community organizing or democracy promotion were often not given visas.

b. Freedom of Peaceful Assembly and Association

Although the constitution provides for freedom of assembly and association, the government severely restricted the exercise of these rights.

Freedom of Assembly

The constitution provides for the right of assembly, but the government continued to curtail this right. A ban on demonstrations in Algiers remained in effect. Authorities utilized the ban during the year to prohibit assembly within the city limits. Authorities required citizens and organizations to obtain permits from the government-appointed local governor before holding public meetings. During the year the government restricted licenses to political parties, NGOs, and other groups to hold indoor rallies or delay permission until the eve of the event, thereby impeding publicity and outreach efforts by organizers. On April 20, Algerian security forces arrested Ali Belhadj at a protest in Tizi Ouzou demanding that the government give the Amazigh (Berber) language official status and recognition

Hotels in Algiers and other major cities continued their historic practice of refusing to sign rental contracts for meeting spaces with political parties, NGOs, and civil associations without a copy of a written authorization from the Ministry of Interior for the proposed gathering.

Throughout the year police dispersed unauthorized gatherings or prevented marching groups of protesters from protesting. Police typically dispersed protestors a few hours after a protest began and arrested and detained organizers for a few hours. On August 31, members of the unregistered local association SOS-Disparus organized a demonstration in collaboration with LADDH at the historic post office in downtown Algiers. Police surrounded the demonstration area, and after one hour dispersed the protestors and arrested the alleged organizers. Detained organizers were released from custody within a few hours.

On March 26, human rights activists and unemployed individuals picketed the annual Ghardaia carpet celebration's opening parade. Police violently dispersed the protest and arrested several protesters.

Freedom of Association

The constitution provides for the right of association, but the government severely restricted this right.

The law grants the government wide-ranging oversight of and influence in the day-to-day activities of civil society organizations. The law requires civil organizations to apply to the Ministry of Interior for permission to operate. Once registered, organizations must inform the government of their activities, funding sources, and personnel, including notification when there are personnel changes. The law imposes an additional requirement that associations obtain government preapproval before accepting foreign funds. If organizations fail to provide required information to the government or attempt to operate with or accept foreign funds without authorization, they are subject to fines between DZD 2,000 and DZD 5,000 ($25 and $63). The law's extensive requirements and uneven enforcement served as major impediments to the development of civil society. The law prohibits formation of a political party with a religious platform, but some political parties were widely known to be Islamist (notably the MSP). The government registered opposition parties that met the law's stringent requirements for political party registration, and during the year registered dozens of new political parties.

Several civil associations, including LADDH, reported difficulty obtaining proper authorizations to hold the "general assembly" required under the law for renewal of accreditation. Foreign organizations seeking accreditation reported significant difficulty completing the registration process.

The January 2012 revision to the law of associations fails to protect the freedom of association consistent with the country's international obligations. The law requires all publications to have prior approval by a media regulatory authority. It also restricts expression and access to information in several major areas, such as national identity, sovereignty, the economy, and national security.

The Ministry of Interior may deny a license to or dissolve any group regarded as a threat to the government's authority or to public order, and on some occasions failed to grant in an expeditious fashion official recognition to NGOs, associations, religious groups, and political parties.

The government issued licenses and subsidies to domestic associations, especially youth, medical, and neighborhood associations. According to the MOI, there were 80,000 registered associations. Of that total, only a few hundred were functioning and credible independent national NGOs.

Despite these legal provisions and the specter of penalties for unauthorized operation, more than 100 unlicensed NGOs, such as women's advocacy groups, charitable organizations, and political advocacy groups focused on atrocities committed in the 1990s, operated openly. Unlicensed NGOs did not receive government assistance, and citizens were at times hesitant to associate with these organizations.

c. Freedom of Religion

See the Department of State's *International Religious Freedom Report* at www.state.gov/j/drl/irf/rpt/.

d. Freedom of Movement, Internally Displaced Persons, Protection of Refugees, and Stateless Persons

The constitution provides for freedom of movement, but the government restricted the exercise of this right.

The government generally cooperated with the UNHCR and other humanitarian organizations in providing protection and assistance to internally displaced persons, refugees, returning refugees, asylum seekers, stateless persons, and other persons of concern.

In-Country Movement: The government maintained restrictions for security reasons on travel into the southern locales of El-Oued and Illizi, near hydrocarbon industry installations and the Libyan border, respectively. The government also prevented overland tourist travel between the southern cities of Djanet and Tamanrasset, citing the threat of terrorism. In the Aboud case, the government hindered the movement of a journalist. The government did not permit young men eligible for the draft who had not yet completed their military service to leave the country without special authorization, although the government granted such authorization to students and persons with special family circumstances, notably those individuals with family members residing in Western Sahara.

Foreign Travel: The family code does not permit those under age 18 to travel abroad without a guardian's permission. Married women under 18 years of age may not travel abroad without permission from their husbands, but married women over age 18 may do so.

Protection of Refugees

Access to Asylum: While the country's laws provide generally for asylum or refugee status, the government has not established a formal system through which displaced persons can request asylum. There were no reports that the government granted refugee status and asylum to new refugee applicants during the year. According to the UNHCR, the government did not accept UNHCR-determined refugee status for individuals from sub-Saharan Africa fleeing conflict, specifically Nigerians, Chadians, Malians, and Nigerians. The UNHCR reported an increase in the number of sub-Saharan Africans (notably Cameroonians) applying for asylum at their offices in Algiers during the year. As of September 10, the office had registered 1,209 asylum cases (totaling 1,365 individuals) and had registered 199 recognized refugees. The majority of the asylum seekers were from Cameroon, Ivory Coast, and Nigeria. The "mandate" refugees were primarily from the Democratic Republic of the Congo, Iraq, and Palestine. The Algiers office also reported that in the last year it successfully resettled 27 refugees: 21 to the United States and six to Sweden. There was no evidence of any pattern of discrimination toward asylum applicants, but the lack of a formal asylum system made this difficult to credibly assess.

According to the UNHCR, as of mid-September, approximately 18, 000 Syrian nationals resided in various cities in the country, of which approximately 500 were registered refugees. More were awaiting registration by the government and the Algerian Red Crescent. The government continued to maintain "welcome facilities" that provided food and shelter for those Syrians without means to support themselves. The facilities were located at a summer camp in the seaside area of Algiers known as Sidi Fredj. The government has imposed visa entry requirements on Syrians and has turned back some individuals at the airport.

Following the outbreak of violence in northern Mali in January, observers including the ICRC and the UNHCR reported an influx of individuals into Algeria across the Malian border inconsistent with traditional migratory movements. Both organizations estimated that as many as 20,000 migrants have been absorbed into local communities in southern Algeria. A small refugee camp managed by the Algerian Red Crescent near the southern city of Bordj Badj Mokhtar housed an estimated 350 individual Malian refugees in September. These numbers, however, have not been verified by the UNHCR since, citing security concerns, the government has not allowed the UNHCR or the international community access to Malian refugees.

Refoulement: The government provided some protection against the expulsion or return of refugees to countries where their lives or freedom would be threatened because of their race, religion, nationality, membership in a particular social group, or political opinion, such as Sahrawi refugees to Western Sahara or Morocco. Authorities did not extend legal protections to asylum seekers from sub-Saharan Africa or Syrians residing in Algiers.

Refugee Abuse: In September authorities in Annaba conducted a security sweep that resulted in the arrest and deportation of approximately 50 sub-Saharan African migrants, some of whom may have been qualified refugees.

Employment: The government did not make a provision for refugee employment. Refugees relied largely on remittances from family, the support of local family and acquaintances, and assistance from the Algerian Red Crescent and international aid organizations.

The government provided protection to an estimated 90,000 to 165,000 Sahrawi refugees who departed Western Sahara after Morocco took control of the territory in the 1970s. The UNHCR, the World Food Program (WFP), the Algerian Red Crescent, the Sahrawi Red Crescent, and other organizations also assisted Sahrawi refugees. Neither the government nor the refugee leadership allowed the UNHCR to conduct a registration or complete a census of the Sahrawi refugees. In the absence of formal registration, UNHCR and WFP humanitarian assistance was based on a planning figure of 90,000 most vulnerable refugees with 35,000 requiring supplemental rations.

Access to Basic Services: Sahrawi refugees lived predominantly in five camps near the city of Tindouf, administered by the Popular Front for the Liberation of the Saguia el Harma and Rio de Oro (Polisario). The remote location of the camps and lack of government presence resulted in lack of access to employment, basic services, education, police, and courts for Sahrawis. Access to basic services for other refugee groups (notably Malians, Syrians, and Nigeriens) remained difficult to assess this year. The government provided free health care to refugee children. The government permitted refugee children to attend school, but refugees and international organizations reported on the difficulty experienced by refugee children in their attempts to integrate into the Algerian education system.

Durable Solutions: The government generally did not accept refugees from third countries for resettlement. The Sahrawi refugees have not sought local integration or naturalization during their 40-year stay in the refugee camps near Tindouf, and their government-in-exile, the Polisario, continued to call for a referendum on independence in Western Sahara. Other refugee groups, predominately Syrian, did not seek resettlement, local integration, or naturalization, expressing an intention to return to their home countries when conditions were stable, or to move on to Europe.

Temporary Protection: The law did not provide formal temporary protection to individuals who may not qualify as refugees, but the government continued its practice of declining to deport migrants expressing a credible fear of return to their home country based on political instability. The government expressed concern over growing numbers of migrants seeking the protection of asylum application without qualifications.

Section 3. Respect for Political Rights: The Right of Citizens to Change Their Government

The constitution provides citizens the right to change their government peacefully, but significantly limited its exercise. Restrictions on freedom of assembly and association, as well as restrictions on political party activities, also limited this right.

Elections and Political Participation

The constitution mandates presidential elections every five years and there are no presidential term limits.

Recent Elections: Dozens of new parties took part in legislative elections held in May 2012. Foreign observers characterized the elections as largely peaceful, but pointed to low voter turnout and a high rate of ballot invalidity. Five hundred international observers (from the European Union, Arab League, National Democratic Institute, and Carter Center, among others) monitored voting and appraised the process as generally favorable, although they criticized the government's refusal to grant access to voter registration lists. Opposition groups claimed widespread fraud. The National Liberation Front (FLN) won the largest number of seats, nearly doubling its share; the National Rally for Democracy (RND) maintained its previous level of representation, thereby leaving the balance of power the same after the elections. Smaller parties (such as the Socialist Workers Party) criticized provisions of the election law that awarded seats only to those parties that won at least 5 percent of the vote and apportioned seats won by parties that received less than that amount to larger, more successful parties. In December elections for the Senate, the upper house of parliament, the RND won the majority of seats. The previously dominant FLN lost seats. Under the law the president is entitled to appoint one-third of the Senate seats, and at year's end he had filled the seats with several former cabinet ministers.

The government officially estimated turnout of the May 2012 parliamentary election at 43 percent, a figure that opposition parties and experts argued was grossly inflated. The Algerian Press Service reported early turnout estimates of 15 percent.

Political Parties: There were no cases during the year of government violence against members of the political opposition. The Ministry of Interior must approve political parties before they can operate legally. On February 19, the ministry notified an Islamist group, the Free Awakening Front, that its license to operate as a political party had been rejected but provided no explanation. Religious Affairs Minister Bouabdallah noted that the Interior Ministry would not license religion-based parties pursuant to the law.

Pursuant to the constitution, all parties must have a "national base." A party must have received 4 percent of the vote or at least 2,000 votes in 25 provinces in one of the last three legislative elections to participate in national elections, making it very difficult to create new political parties. It is illegal for parties to be based upon religion, ethnicity, gender, language, or region.

The law does not place significant restrictions on voter registration, but implementation of voter registration and identification laws proved inconsistent and confusing during elections held during the year. In its report on the May legislative elections, the National Democratic Institute highlighted confusion over identification requirements.

Membership in the Islamic Salvation Front, a political party banned since 1992, remained illegal. The law also bans political party ties to nonpolitical associations and regulates party financing and reporting requirements. According to the law, political parties cannot receive direct or indirect financial or material support from any foreign parties. The law also stipulates that resources are collected from contributions of the party's members, donations, and revenue from its activities, in addition to possible state funding.

Participation of Women and Minorities: The law requires that the government promote political rights for women by encouraging increased female representation within elected assemblies. The law mandates that 30 percent of all candidates on electoral tickets be women. In accordance with this amendment, of the 462 candidates elected to parliament in May 2012, 147 were women, increasing their rate of representation from 8 percent in 2007 to 31 percent in 2012.

Three women held seats in the cabinet, a woman led the Workers Party, and three major political parties – the FLN, National Rally for Democracy, and RCD – had women's divisions headed by women. Only four of Algeria's 1,514 mayors were women.

The ethnic Amazigh (Berber) population of approximately 10 million participated freely and actively in the political process and represented one-third of the government.

Section 4. Corruption and Lack of Transparency in Government

Corruption: The law provides for criminal penalties of two to 10 years in prison for official corruption. Corruption remained a problem as reflected in World Bank governance data.

In May the Ministry of Finance's Central Office for the Suppression of Corruption began operations.

Whistleblower Protection: A new law protects whistleblowers. Penalties for breach of this law (commission of acts of vengeance and intimidation) include imprisonment between six months and five years and fines ranging from DZD 50,000 to 500,000 ($625 to $6250). Whistleblowers determined by a judicial authority to have made "abusive" accusations face the same potential penalties, which had a chilling effect on potential whistleblowers who were unable to determine whether a denunciation might be considered slanderous.

Financial Disclosure: The law does not require elected and senior officials to declare their assets and provides parliamentary immunity in certain cases. Nevertheless, presidential decrees published in 2006 make high-level government officials subject to other financial disclosure laws. The decrees also stipulated the formation of an anticorruption agency, which the government formed by year's end. Corruption throughout the government stemmed largely from the bloated nature of the bureaucracy and a lack of transparent oversight. Government contracts for housing in particular were often not enforced, and government-subsidized housing units were often of substandard construction as a result.

Public Access to Information: Lack of government transparency remained a serious problem. Most ministries had websites, but not all were regularly maintained to provide updated information.

Section 5. Governmental Attitude Regarding International and Nongovernmental Investigation of Alleged Violations of Human Rights

A variety of domestic human rights groups operated with varying degrees of government restriction. The law requires all civil associations to apply for operating permission and at year's end a few major civil associations (notably SOS-Disparu) remained unrecognized but tolerated. During the year no human rights organization complained of government monitoring or infiltration.

AI and other organizations, such as the AFL-CIO Solidarity Center, reported that historical problems with visas for non-Algerian employees remained an issue.

LADDH, a legally recognized NGO with members throughout the country and independent funding, was the most active independent human rights group. The smaller Algerian League for Human Rights, a separate organization based in Constantine, was licensed, and members throughout the country monitored individual cases.

By law NGOs not legally recognized by the Ministry of Interior can conduct human rights investigations. Although organizations themselves are generally not granted access to prisons for monitoring, the National Commission on Prisons includes representatives from many large NGOs, including NADA. These commissioners report their findings freely.

UN and Other International Bodies: The UN Working Group on Enforced or Involuntary Disappearances continued its work but released no public findings or statements this year. The government continued to deny requests for visits from the UN special rapporteur on torture (pending since 1997), the UN special rapporteur on extrajudicial executions (pending since 1998), the UN special rapporteur on human rights and counterterrorism (pending since 2006), and the UN special rapporteur on arbitrary detention (pending since 2009).

Section 6. Discrimination, Societal Abuses, and Trafficking in Persons

The constitution prohibits discrimination based on birth, race, gender, language, and social status. The government effectively enforced the law, although women continued to face legal and social discrimination.

Women

Rape and Domestic Violence: Rape, both spousal and nonspousal, occurred. The law criminalizes nonspousal rape but does not address spousal rape. Prison sentences for nonspousal rape range from one to five years, and authorities generally enforced the law. Claims filed by women for rape and sexual abuse continued to face judicial obstacles, and many women did not report incidents of rape because of societal pressures and bureaucratic problems in securing convictions. On November 21, news outlets reported statistics provided by the director of the judicial police Office for the Protection of Childhood, Juvenile Delinquency, and the Protection of Women Victims of Violence. The director indicated that in the first nine months of the year, 266 women were victims of rape, sexual harassment, and incest, and that cases were reported in each of Algeria's 48 provinces. She further indicated that she believed the actual incidence of these crimes was more widespread than the figure suggested because reporting rape and other sexual violence remained "taboo" in Algerian culture. She added that women "prefer to suffer the pain in silence" rather than face possible rejection by their families and societies, particularly in those cases where sexual violence resulted in pregnancy.

Domestic violence was widespread. The penal code states that a person must be "incapacitated" for 15 days and a woman claiming domestic abuse must visit a "forensic physician" for an examination to document injuries. The physician then provides the survivor with a "certificate of incapacity" attesting to the injuries. The survivor then presents the certificate to authorities as the basis of the criminal complaint.

In March the gendarmerie reported that 6,039 women were the victims of domestic violence in 2012.

Harmful Traditional Practices: There was one alleged honor killing during the year. According to media reports, a man was arrested on June 5 for killing five people to "cleanse his family's honor" after his niece eloped with her boyfriend to avoid an arranged marriage. There were no human rights organizations in the country that focused on honor crimes, but international organizations gathered information about the practice. The law provides a "crime of passion" defense to both men and women who discover their spouses engaged in the act of adultery, which lessens the punishment of the perpetrator. The provisions of the law limit the defense to lawfully married spouses.

Sexual Harassment: The punishment for sexual harassment is one to two years' imprisonment and a fine of DZD 50,000 to DZD 100,000 ($625 to $1250). The punishment is doubled for a second offense. The majority of reported cases of harassment occurred in the workplace. In January an appellate court affirmed the conviction of former television station director Said Lamrani for sexual harassment and increased the damages assessed by the court of first instance from DZD 30,000 to DZD 300,000 ($375 to $3,750) per victim plus an additional fine of DZD 300,000 ($3,750).

Reproductive Rights: The government did not impose restrictions on the right of couples and individuals to decide the number, timing, and spacing of their children. Married and unmarried women alike had access to contraceptives. According to a study conducted in 2009 by the health ministry, 62 percent of women, most of them married, reported regular use of contraceptives. Women encountered social and family pressure that restricted them from making independent decisions about their health and reproductive rights.

Discrimination: Although the constitution provides for gender equality, many aspects of the law and traditional social practices discriminate against women. In addition religious extremists advocated practices that led to restrictions on women's behavior, including freedom of movement. In some rural regions women faced extreme social pressure to veil as a precondition for freedom of movement and employment. The family code contains traditional elements of Islamic law. The family code prohibits Muslim women from marrying non-Muslims, although authorities did not always enforce this regulation. Muslim men may marry non-Muslim women. A woman may marry a foreigner and transmit citizenship and nationality to both her children and spouse.

Women can seek divorce for irreconcilable differences and violation of a prenuptial agreement. In a divorce the law provides for the wife to retain the family's home until children reach 18 years of age. Custody of children normally is awarded to the mother, but she may not make decisions about education or take the children out of the country without the father's authorization. Women were more likely to retain the family's home if they had custody of the children.

The family code affirms the religiously based practice of allowing a man to marry as many as four wives. According to the family code, polygyny is only permitted upon the permission of the first wife and the determination of a judge as to the husband's financial ability to support an additional wife. Polygyny occurred in 1 to 2 percent of marriages. It was unclear whether authorities followed the law in all cases.

Amendments to the family code supersede the religiously based requirement that a male sponsor consent to the marriage of a woman. The sponsor represents the woman during the religious or civil ceremony. Although this requirement has been formally retained and the sponsor continues to contract the marriage, the woman may choose any man that she wishes to be her sponsor. Some families subjected women to virginity tests before marriage.

Women suffered from discrimination in inheritance claims and were entitled to a smaller portion of an estate than male children or a deceased husband's brothers. Women did not often have exclusive control over assets that they brought to a marriage or that they earned. Married women may take out business loans and use their own financial resources. Women enjoy rights equal to those of men in regard to property ownership, and women landowners' names are listed on property titles.

Women faced discrimination in employment. Leaders of women's organizations reported that discrimination was common and women were less likely to receive equal pay for equal work or receive promotions. In urban areas there was social encouragement for women to pursue higher education and/or a career. Girls graduated from high school more frequently than boys.

According to 2010 statistics, women represented 55 percent of the medical profession, 60 percent of the media profession, 30 percent of the upper levels of the legal profession, and more than 60 percent of the education profession. In addition 36 percent of judges were women. Women served at all levels in the judicial system, and female police officers were added to some precincts to assist women with abuse claims. Of nine million workers nationally, two million were female. Women may own businesses, enter into contracts, and pursue careers similar to those of men. Nevertheless, women faced challenges with regard to access to credit and businesses.

Children

Birth registration: Citizenship and nationality are transmitted from the mother or father. Under the law children born to a Muslim father are Muslim, regardless of the mother's religion.

Education: Education was free, compulsory, and universal through the secondary level to age 17. Treatment and attendance of girls and boys was equal throughout the education system.

Child Abuse: Child abuse is illegal but continued to be a problem. Experts assumed that many cases went unreported because of family reticence. According to NADA, 1,300 cases of child abduction and disappearance were reported during the year. Organized crime was responsible, as well as family conflict that resulted in parental abduction. Kidnapping for any reason is a crime. Laws prohibiting parental abduction do not penalize mothers and fathers differently.

Sexual Exploitation of Children: The criminal code prohibits solicitation for prostitution and stipulates prison sentences of between 10 and 20 years when the offense is committed against a minor under the age of 18 years. According to the law, the age for consensual sex is 16 years. The law stipulates a prison sentence of between 10 and 20 years for rape when the victim is a minor. Authorities rarely carried out this sentence. The law prohibits pornography and establishes prison sentences of between two months and two years as well as fines up to DZD 2,000 ($25).

International Child Abductions: The country is not a party to the 1980 Hague Convention on the Civil Aspects of International Child Abduction.

Anti-Semitism

The country's Jewish population numbered fewer than 1,000 persons, and local Jewish community leaders estimated the number to be in the low hundreds. There were no functioning synagogues. No derogatory political cartoons or articles directed at the Jewish community were published during the year. In July television stations across the Arab world, including Algerian satellite station Atlas TV, aired an historical mini-series for Ramadan called "Khayber." The Anti-Defamation League criticized the mini-series as being anti-Semitic. The government did not promote anti-bias education, and there is no hate crime legislation.

Trafficking in Persons

See the Department of State's *Trafficking in Persons Report* at www.state.gov/j/tip/.

Persons with Disabilities

The law prohibits discrimination against persons with disabilities in employment, education, access to health care, or the provision of other state services, although the government did not effectively enforce these provisions. Persons with disabilities faced widespread social discrimination. Few government buildings were accessible to persons with disabilities. Public enterprises that downsized generally ignored a requirement that they reserve 1 percent of jobs for persons with disabilities. Social security provided payments for orthopedic equipment. The Ministry of National Solidarity (MNS) provided some financial support to health-care-oriented NGOs, but for many NGOs such financial support represented approximately 2 percent of their budgets.

The MNS maintained that there were two million individuals with disabilities in the country, of whom the largest percentages were classified as "chronically ill" or "other" (38 and 30 percent, respectively). According to the Algerian Federation of Wheelchair Associations, however, there were three million persons with disabilities living in the country. The government estimated that approximately 44 percent of citizens with disabilities had some form of motor disability, 32 percent had communication difficulties, and 24 percent suffered from a visual disability. The government classified approximately 193,000 individuals as "fully disabled" and claimed during the year to have appropriated DZD 9.54 billion ($123 million) for their welfare.

Societal Abuses, Discrimination, and Acts of Violence Based on Sexual Orientation and Gender Identity

The penal code criminalizes public consensual same-sex sexual relations for men and women, and there is no specific legal protection for lesbian, gay, bisexual, and transgender (LGBT) persons. The law stipulates penalties that include imprisonment of two months to two years and fines of DZD 500 to DZD 2,000 ($6 to $25). If a minor is involved, the adult may face up to three years' imprisonment and a fine of DZD 10,000 ($125). There were no known prosecutions for same-sex relations during the year.

Existing laws on associations may be used to refuse full legal standing to LGBT associations. LGBT persons faced societal discrimination. Some LGBT individuals received violent threats and felt compelled to flee the country. While some LGBT persons lived openly, the vast majority did not, and most feared reprisal from their families or harassment from authorities. In September 31 an LGBT activist using the pseudonym Zak Ostmane told Parisian daily *Le Monde* that after publishing a "manifesto for homosexuality" on his Facebook page, which Algiers news website Algerie Focus subsequently reprinted, he rarely left his house for fear of reprisals.

Abu Nawas, an Algiers-based LGBT advocacy group, continued cyber-activism on behalf of the LGBT community. Oran-based LGBT association Alouen began a series of LGBT-themed podcasts in July published on the association's Facebook and YouTube pages. Both organizations reported that members of the Algerian LGBT community declined to report cases of homophobic abuse and rape for fear of reprisal by authorities. Both organizations also reported that access to health services could be difficult because medical personnel often treated LGBT patients "unprofessionally."

On May 4, Algiers daily *El Khabar* reported that two homosexual men had been arrested and placed in pretrial detention in Oran on charges of indecent conduct and incitement to immorality after both changed their Facebook relationship status to "married." They were released on May 7 after a preliminary hearing and were awaiting trial.

Other Societal Violence or Discrimination

HIV/AIDS was widely considered a shameful disease in the country. Since 1998 the government has offered free antiretroviral treatment to all persons who were eligible. New HIV infections among children have been virtually eliminated. There were 61 centers offering free testing services to detect HIV/AIDS. Only 51 percent of women, single and married, noted use of condoms to prevent infection.

According to Ministry of Health statistics, as of August approximately 7,300 persons were either HIV-positive or living with AIDS. In 2011 the NGO National Foundation for Health Promotion and Research Development released a study indicating 12,000 citizens were infected with AIDS.

On August 11, LADDH issued a communique denouncing the government's failure to include traditional Berber names among those authorized to be included on birth certificates. The following week the Ministry of Interior released a list of 300 approved Berber names, but in Arabic script. LADDH requested the intervention of the UN special rapporteur for Racism, Racial Intolerance, Xenophobia, and Intolerance, the special rapporteur for Human Rights, and the special rapporteur for Cultural Rights.

Section 7. Worker Rights

a. Freedom of Association and the Right to Collective Bargaining

The constitution provides workers with the right to join and form unions of their choice provided they are citizens. The country ratified the International Labor Organization's (ILO's) conventions on freedom of association and collective bargaining but failed to enact legislation needed to fully implement these conventions.

The law requires that workers obtain government approval to form a union, and the Ministry of Labor must approve or disapprove a union application within 30 days. The law also provides for the creation of independent unions, although the union's membership must account for at least 20 percent of an enterprise's workforce. Although unions have the right to form and join federations or confederations, the government only recognized the General Union of Algerian Workers, which represented a majority of public sector workers. Unions may recruit members at the workplace. The law prohibits discrimination by employers against union members and organizers and provides mechanisms for resolving trade union complaints of antiunion practices by employers.

The law permits unions to affiliate with international labor bodies and to develop relations with foreign labor groups. For example, the General Union of Algerian Workers (UGTA) is a member of the International Confederation of Free Trade Unions. Nevertheless, the law prohibits unions from associating with political parties and also prohibits unions from receiving funds from foreign sources. The courts are empowered to dissolve unions that engage in illegal activities. The government may invalidate a union's legal status if its objectives are perceived by authorities as contrary to the established institutional system, public order, good morals, or the laws or regulations in force.

The law provides for collective bargaining for all unions, and the government permitted the exercise of this right for authorized unions. Nevertheless, the UGTA remained the only union authorized to negotiate collective bargaining agreements.

The law provides for the right to strike, and workers exercised this right, subject to conditions. Striking requires a secret ballot of the whole workforce. The government can restrict strikes on a number of grounds, including economic crisis, obstruction of public services, or possibility of subversive actions. Furthermore, due to the emergency law in force, all public demonstrations, including protests and strikes, must receive prior government authorization. According to the law, workers may strike only after 14 days of mandatory conciliation or mediation. On occasion the government offered to mediate disputes. The law states that decisions reached in mediation are binding on both parties. If no agreement is reached in mediation, the workers may strike legally after they vote by secret ballot to do so. The law requires that a minimum level of essential public services must be maintained during public-sector service strikes. The ILO noted that the list of essential services was broad and included services such as banking, radio, and television. The ILO expressed concern regarding what it deemed excessive penalties ranging from eight days to two months' imprisonment imposed by the government on workers participating in peaceful strikes.

No new independent unions formed during the year, although unions representing secondary school teachers and gas workers were invited to resolve unspecified discrepancies in their applications. Many trade unions were not recognized, as the government interfered with their attempts to register. Attempts by new unions to form federations or confederations also were obstructed by administrative maneuvers in which processing registration requests were delayed. Since 1996 the Autonomous Unions Confederation (SNAPAP), which functions without official status, repeatedly attempted to organize independent unions, without success. The government did not allow SNAPAP to register as a national confederation, thus preventing it from establishing an independent multi-sector confederation that would include private sector employees. SNAPAP and other independent unions faced government interference throughout the year, including official obstruction of general assembly meetings and police harassment during sit-in protests. Furthermore, unions in multinational companies, specifically in oil and gas production, were virtually nonexistent due to antiunion practices and threats and harassment by employers. The government also sought to weaken independent unions by forming union clones to discredit the actual organizations.

Antiunion intimidation was commonplace, and there were several strikes launched in reaction to the government's refusal to extend official recognition to fledgling new unions and its practice of only engaging with the UGTA.

The national union of health workers conducted a series of planned, announced strikes throughout the summer months to protest low salaries and prohibitions on "moonlighting." The union specifically denounced disciplinary measures taken against doctors who worked in private clinics outside of their hours at government hospitals. Officials accused the moonlighting doctors of stealing supplies from public hospitals for use at private clinics.

In August the national union of postal workers conducted a five-day strike to demand a 30 percent salary increase. The strike impacted all sectors of society, largely based on the central role of post offices in retail banking.

b. Prohibition of Forced or Compulsory Labor

The constitution prohibits all forms of forced or compulsory labor, but there were reports from the Ministry of Labor and NGOs that such practices occurred. Forced labor conditions existed for migrant workers, who were not fully protected by labor law. Construction workers and female domestic workers were reportedly vulnerable.

See the Department of State's *Trafficking in Persons Report* at www.state.gov/j/tip/.

c. Prohibition of Child Labor and Minimum Age for Employment

The law prohibits participation by minors in dangerous, unhealthy, or harmful work or in work that is considered inappropriate because of social and religious considerations. The minimum legal age for employment is 16 years, but children that are younger may work as apprentices with permission from their parents or legal guardian. The law prohibits minors from working in dangerous or harmful work, but it does not establish a list of hazardous occupations prohibited to minors, nor does it cover work in the informal sector which, according to official estimates, more than doubled in size to nearly four million workers. Approximately half of those working in the informal sector were under age 30.

Although specific data was unavailable, child labor reportedly occurred primarily in the agriculture and construction sectors, as well as in the informal sector, where children worked as domestic servants.

The Ministry of Labor is responsible for enforcing child labor laws. Authorities enforced the law in a limited way. The ministry conducted and in some cases investigated companies suspected of hiring underage workers. Monitoring and enforcement practices for child labor were not consistent and were hampered by an insufficient number of inspectors.

d. Acceptable Conditions of Work

A tripartite social pact among business, government, and the official union established the national minimum wage of DZD 15,000 ($188) per month in 2009. This did not provide a decent standard of living for a worker and family. Families making only DZD 8,000 ($100) per month were considered to be living in poverty.

The standard workweek was 40 hours, including one hour for lunch per day. Employees who worked longer than the standard workweek received premium pay on a sliding scale from time-and-a-half to double-time, depending on whether the overtime occurred on a normal workday, a weekend, or a holiday.

The law contains occupational health and safety standards, which were not fully enforced. There were no known reports of workers being dismissed for removing themselves from hazardous working conditions. If workers face such conditions, they reserve the right to renegotiate their contract or, failing that, resort to the courts. While this legal mechanism exists, the high demand for employment in the country gave an advantage to employers seeking to exploit employees. Economic migrants from sub-Saharan Africa and elsewhere working in the country without legal immigration status were not protected by the country's labor standards, making them vulnerable to exploitation. The labor law does not adequately cover migrant workers who are primarily employed in construction and as domestic workers.

In general the Ministry of Labor enforced labor standards, including ensuring compliance with the minimum wage regulation and safety standards. Nevertheless, broad enforcement remained ineffective and insufficient.